INTERMEDIATE SET #1

RUDIMENTS EXAM SERIES

By Glory St. Germain ARCT RMT MYCC UMTC
Shelagh McKibbon-U'Ren RMT UMTC

ULTIMATE
MUSIC THEORY

GSG MUSIC

Enriching Lives Through Music Education

ISBN: 978-1-927641-04-0

The Ultimate Music Theory™ Program
Enriching Lives Through Music Education

The Ultimate Music Theory™ Workbooks & Answer Books Program includes:

UMT Rudiments Workbooks for Prep 1, Prep 2, Basic, Intermediate, Advanced & Complete
UMT Exam Series (Set #1 & Set #2) for Preparatory, Basic, Intermediate & Advanced

Supplemental Workbooks for PREP LEVEL, LEVELS 1 - 8 & COMPLETE LEVEL
UMT Supplemental Exam Series for LEVEL 5, LEVEL 6, LEVEL 7 & LEVEL 8

The Ultimate Music Theory Program is the *Way to Score Success* as UMT helps students prepare for nationally recognized theory examinations including the Royal Conservatory of Music.

 Library and Archives Canada Cataloguing in Publication. UMT Workbooks & Exam Series /Glory St. Germain & Shelagh McKibbon-U'Ren. Respect Copyright. All rights reserved. GlorylandPublishing.com

Ultimate Music Theory Rudiments Exam Series

GP - EPS1	ISBN: 978-1-927641-00-2	Preparatory Rudiments Exams Set #1
GP - EPS1A	ISBN: 978-1-927641-08-8	Preparatory Exams Answers Set #1
GP - EPS2	ISBN: 978-1-927641-01-9	Preparatory Rudiments Exams Set #2
GP - EPS2A	ISBN: 978-1-927641-09-5	Preparatory Exams Answers Set #2
GP - EBS1	ISBN: 978-1-927641-02-6	Basic Rudiments Exams Set #1
GP - EBS1A	ISBN: 978-1-927641-10-1	Basic Exams Answers Set #1
GP - EBS2	ISBN: 978-1-927641-03-3	Basic Rudiments Exams Set #2
GP - EBS2A	ISBN: 978-1-927641-11-8	Basic Exams Answers Set #2
GP - EIS1	ISBN: 978-1-927641-04-0	Intermediate Rudiments Exams Set #1
GP - EIS1A	ISBN: 978-1-927641-12-5	Intermediate Exams Answers Set #1
GP - EIS2	ISBN: 978-1-927641-05-7	Intermediate Rudiments Exams Set #2
GP - EIS2A	ISBN: 978-1-927641-13-2	Intermediate Exams Answers Set #2
GP - EAS1	ISBN: 978-1-927641-06-4	Advanced Rudiments Exams Set #1
GP - EAS1A	ISBN: 978-1-927641-14-9	Advanced Exams Answers Set #1
GP - EAS2	ISBN: 978-1-927641-07-1	Advanced Rudiments Exams Set #2
GP - EAS2A	ISBN: 978-1-927641-15-6	Advanced Exams Answers Set #2

Ultimate Music Theory Supplemental Exam Series

GP-L5E	ISBN: 978-1-990358-11-1	LEVEL 5 Exams
GP-L5EA	ISBN: 978-1-990358-12-8	LEVEL 5 Exams Answers
GP-L6E	ISBN: 978-1-990358-13-5	LEVEL 6 Exams
GP-L6EA	ISBN: 978-1-990358-14-2	LEVEL 6 Exams Answers
GP-L7E	ISBN: 978-1-990358-15-9	LEVEL 7 Exams
GP-L7EA	ISBN: 978-1-990358-16-6	LEVEL 7 Exams Answers
GP-L8E	ISBN: 978-1-990358-17-3	LEVEL 8 Exams
GP-L8EA	ISBN: 978-1-990358-18-0	LEVEL 8 Exams Answers

Go to UltimateMusicTheory.com **and check out the FREE Resources**

Ultimate Music Theory FREE RESOURCES created just for you!

The **Ultimate Music Theory Exams** reinforce the **UMT Intermediate Rudiments Workbook** and prepare students for continued learning with UMT Advanced Rudiments.

Intermediate Rudiments Theory Examination requirements include Basic Rudiments requirements plus the following:

Pitch
- Double sharps and double flats

Rhythm
- Note and rest time values (breve, whole, half, quarter, eighth, sixteenth and thirty-second)
- Double dotted notes
- Time Signatures in Simple Time and in Compound Time
- Irregular groups in Simple Time (quintuplets and septuplets)

Scales in Major and minor keys up to and including seven sharps and seven flats
- Write or identify: Major and minor (natural, harmonic and melodic) scales, ascending and descending
- Write or identify: Related keys: relative Major and minor, tonic (parallel) Major and minor; enharmonic Major and minor
- Write or identify: Technical degree names of the scale degrees
- Write or identify: Whole-tone scales and chromatic scales (using any standard version)
- Identify: blues scales, Major pentatonic scales, minor pentatonic scales and octatonic scales

Triads in all Major and harmonic minor keys
- Write: Solid (blocked) in Root Position and inversions (close position only)
- Identify: Solid (blocked) or broken in Root Position and inversions (close position or open position)

Intervals - Perfect, Major and minor
- Write or identify: above or below a given note, all intervals and their inversions up to and including an octave, melodic or harmonic form (with or without a Key Signature)

Recognition of Key Signatures up to and including seven sharps and seven flats
- Identify the key (Major or minor) of a given melody with a Key Signature
- Rewrite the excerpt using the correct Key Signature and identify the key (Major or minor)

Transposition (Major Keys up to and including seven sharps and seven flats)
- Transpose a melody up or down any interval within the octave

Cadences in all Major and harmonic minor keys
- Identify cadences in keyboard style only in a musical excerpt
- Perfect (Authentic): V - I (Major) and V - i (minor); Plagal: IV - I (Major) and iv - i (minor); Imperfect (Half Cadence): I - V or IV - V (Major) and i - V or iv - V (minor)

Musical Terms and Signs
- Recognize, define or supply the musical terms or signs as listed in the Intermediate Rudiments Workbook

Analysis
- Analyze a short musical composition, identifying any of the above theory requirements

Score:
  60 - 69 Pass; 70 - 79 Honors; 80 - 89 First Class Honors; 90 - 100 First Class Honors with Distinction

Ultimate Music Theory: *The Way to Score Success!*

UltimateMusicTheory.com © Copyright 2013 Gloryland Publishing. All Rights Reserved.

ULTIMATE MUSIC THEORY
INTERMEDIATE EXAM SET #1 - EXAM #1

Total Score: ____ / 100

> ♪ **UMT Tip:** Before beginning your exam, write out the Circle of Fifths. Write the order of flats and sharps. Write the Major keys on the outside of the circle and the relative minor keys on the inside of the circle.

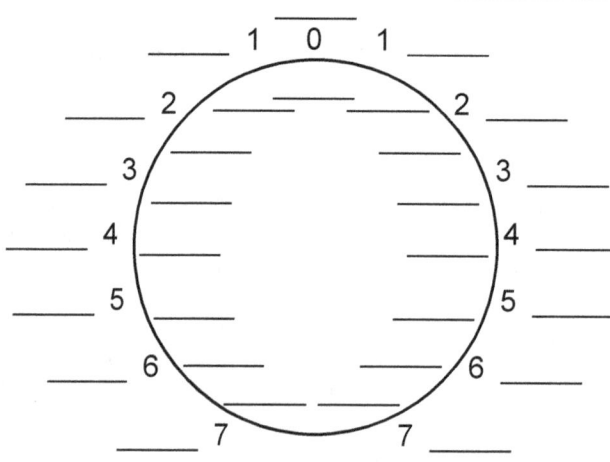

> ♪ **UMT Tip:** Intervals can be inverted by moving the upper (top) note down an octave or by moving the lower (bottom) note up an octave.

1. a) Write the following harmonic intervals below each of the given notes. Use whole notes.

/10

    diminished 2   minor 7   Augmented 5   Major 6   Perfect 8

b) Invert the above harmonic intervals in the given clef. Name the inversions.

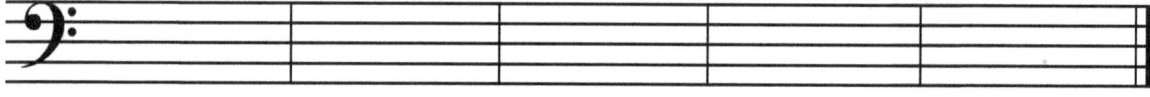

UltimateMusicTheory.com © Copyright 2013 Gloryland Publishing. All Rights Reserved.

ULTIMATE MUSIC THEORY
INTERMEDIATE EXAM SET #1 - EXAM #1

♪ **UMT Tip:** The Dominant triad of a minor key contains the raised 7th (Leading Note).

2. a) Write the following solid triads in close position in the Treble Clef. Use the correct Key Signature and any necessary accidentals. Use whole notes.

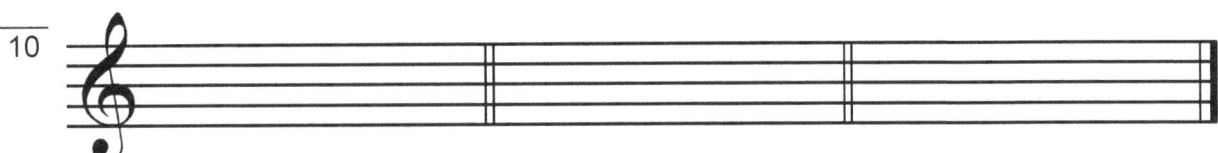

10

      Supertonic triad of   Dominant triad of   Mediant triad of
      A Major   b flat minor harmonic   E flat Major
      in second inversion   in root position   in first inversion

b) Write the following solid triads in close position in the Bass Clef. Use accidentals. Use whole notes.

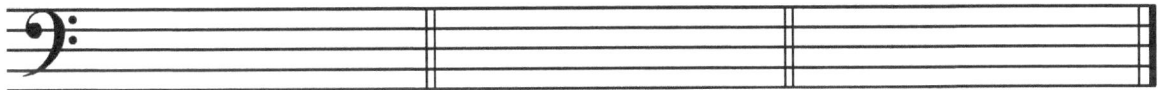

      Subdominant triad of   Dominant triad of   Submediant triad of
      g sharp minor harmonic   c minor harmonic   E Major
      in first inversion   in second inversion   in root position

♪ **UMT Tip:** The quality/type of a triad is whether the triad is Major or minor. The quality/type is based on the Major scale of the root note.

c) Identify the root note and the quality/type of each of the following open position triads.

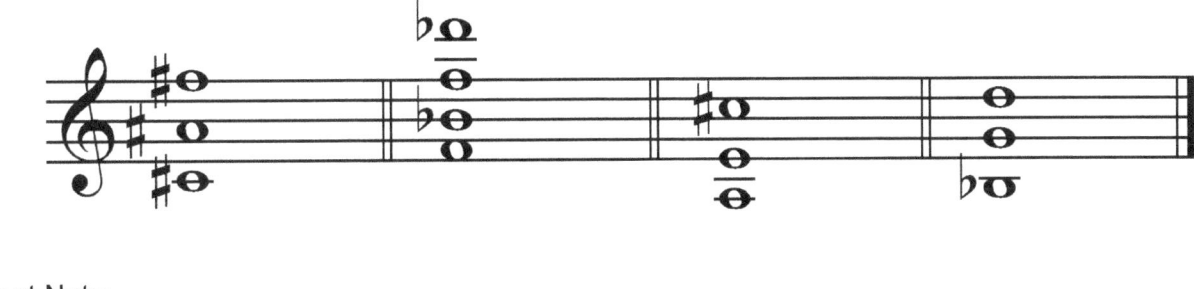

Root Note: _____ _____ _____ _____

Quality/Type: _____ _____ _____ _____

UltimateMusicTheory.com © Copyright 2013 Gloryland Publishing. All Rights Reserved.

ULTIMATE MUSIC THEORY
INTERMEDIATE EXAM SET #1 - EXAM #1

> ♪ **UMT Tip:** Draw a staff in the margin. Write the interval above the Tonic note of the given melody. The top note names the new key.

3. The following melody is in the key of D flat Major.
   a) Transpose the given melody UP an Augmented third. Use the correct Key Signature.
   b) Name the key of the new melody.

Key: D flat Major

Key: _____

> ♪ **UMT Tip:** Name the accidentals in order of the Key Signature. When accidentals are in the correct Key Signature order, the key is usually Major.

The following melody has been written using accidentals instead of a Key Signature.
   c) Name the key of the given melody.
   d) Rewrite the given melody using the correct Key Signature and any necessary accidentals.

Key: _____

ULTIMATE MUSIC THEORY
INTERMEDIATE EXAM SET #1 - EXAM #1

> ♪ **UMT Tip:** Scales may be written with or without a center bar line after the highest note. Either way is correct.

4. Write the following scales, ascending and descending, using the correct Key Signature and any necessary accidentals for each. Use whole notes.

$\overline{10}$ a) f sharp minor natural scale in the Treble Clef.

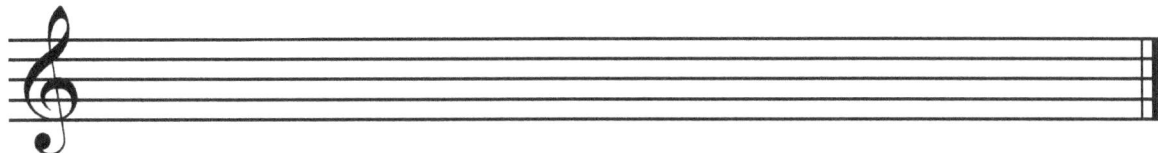

b) C sharp Major scale in the Bass Clef.

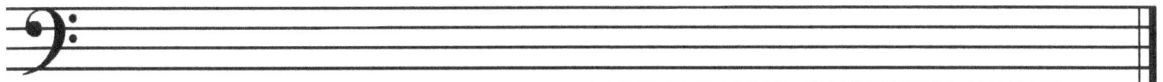

c) relative minor scale, harmonic form, of D flat Major in the Bass Clef.

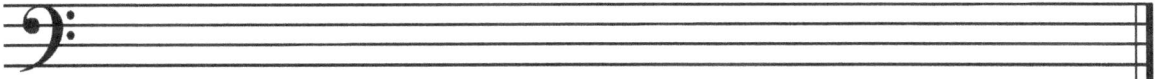

d) Tonic Major scale of f sharp minor in the Treble Clef.

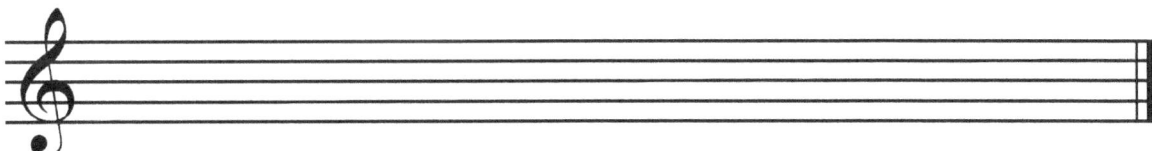

e) Enharmonic Tonic minor scale, melodic form, of e flat minor in the Bass Clef.

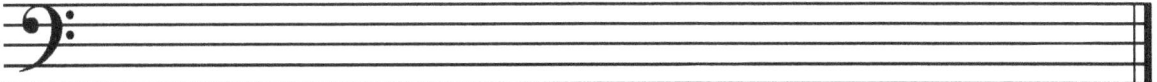

ULTIMATE MUSIC THEORY
INTERMEDIATE EXAM SET #1 - EXAM #1

> ♪ **UMT Tip:** The final note in the Bass Clef can be either the Tonic or Dominant note of the Major or relative minor key.

5. For each of the following cadences, name:
   a) the key.
   b) the type of cadence (Perfect, Plagal or Imperfect).

Key: _____ _____ _____

Type: _____ _____ _____

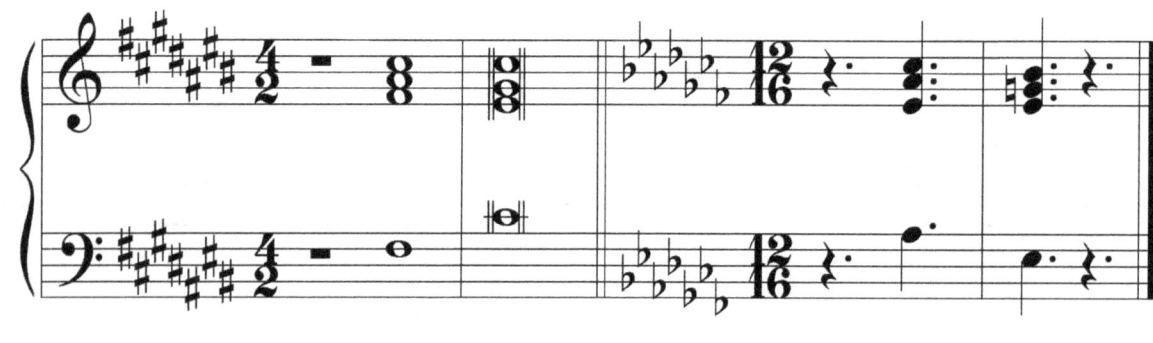

Key: _____ _____

Type: _____ _____

ULTIMATE MUSIC THEORY
INTERMEDIATE EXAM SET #1 - EXAM #1

♪ **UMT Tip:** A musical excerpt does not always start or end on the Tonic note.

6. For each of the following excerpts:
   a) Name the key.
   b) Add the correct Time Signature below the bracket.

Key: _____

Key: _____

Key: _____

Key: _____

Key: _____

ULTIMATE MUSIC THEORY
INTERMEDIATE EXAM SET #1 - EXAM #1

♪ **UMT Tip:**	Write the Basic Beat and the Pulse below each measure. Cross off the Basic Beat as each beat is completed.

7. Add rests below each bracket to complete each measure.

___
10

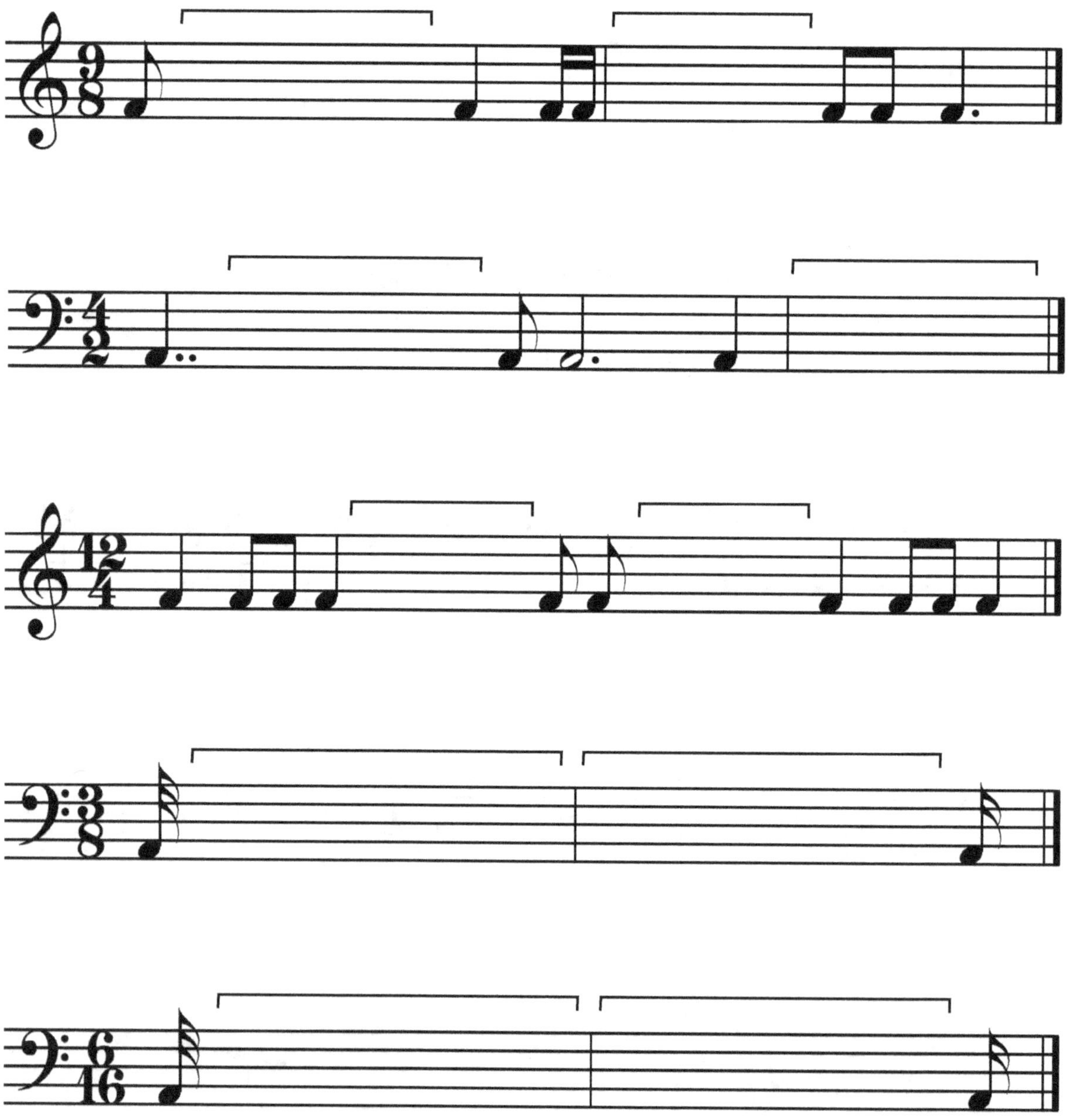

ULTIMATE MUSIC THEORY
INTERMEDIATE EXAM SET #1 - EXAM #1

> ♪ **UMT Tip:** Identify the distances between the notes to find the pattern.

8. a) Name the following scales as blues, chromatic, Major pentatonic, minor pentatonic, octatonic or whole tone.

10

b) For the following Major Key Signatures, identify the technical degree name of each note.

ULTIMATE MUSIC THEORY
INTERMEDIATE EXAM SET #1 - EXAM #1

> ♪ **UMT Tip:** Before looking at the possible definitions, look at the Term and identify the definition. Then match the definition with one of the given definitions.

9. Match each musical term with its English definition. (Not all definitions will be used.)

Term   **Definition**

Term		Definition
spiritoso	_____	a) slow and solemn
troppo	_____	b) without
vivace	_____	c) too much
grave	_____	d) with
fortepiano	_____	e) quiet, tranquil
senza	_____	f) one string; depress the left (piano) pedal
loco	_____	g) three strings; release the left (piano) pedal
con	_____	h) spirited
una corda	_____	i) return to the normal register
tranquillo	_____	j) loud, then suddenly soft
		k) lively, brisk

ULTIMATE MUSIC THEORY
INTERMEDIATE EXAM SET #1 - EXAM #1

> ♪ **UMT Tip:** When identifying the Key Signature, a minor key will usually have an accidental on the raised 7th note - the Leading note.

10. Analyze the following piece of music by answering the questions below.

I Don't Want to Go to Bed!

S. McKibbon

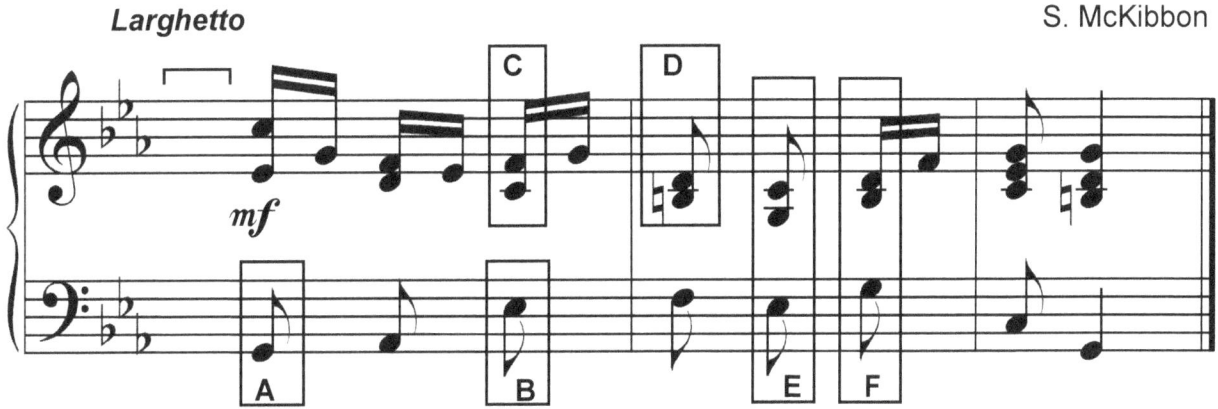

a) Name the key of this piece. _____

b) Explain the tempo of this piece. _____

c) Add the Time Signature directly on the music.

d) Identify the technical degree name of the note at the letter **A**. _____

e) Identify the technical degree name of the note at the letter **B**. _____

f) Name the interval at the letter **C**. _____

g) Name the interval at the letter **D**. _____

h) For the triad at **E**, name: Root: ____ Type/Quality: _____ Position: _____

i) For the triad at **F**, name: Root: ____ Type/Quality: _____ Position: _____

j) Identify the cadence in measure 3 as Perfect, Imperfect or Plagal. _____

UltimateMusicTheory.com © Copyright 2013 Gloryland Publishing. All Rights Reserved.

ULTIMATE MUSIC THEORY
INTERMEDIATE EXAM SET #1 - EXAM #2

Total Score: ____ / 100

> ♪ **UMT Tip:** Before beginning your exam, write out the Circle of Fifths. Write the order of flats and sharps. Write the Major keys on the outside of the circle and the relative minor keys on the inside of the circle.

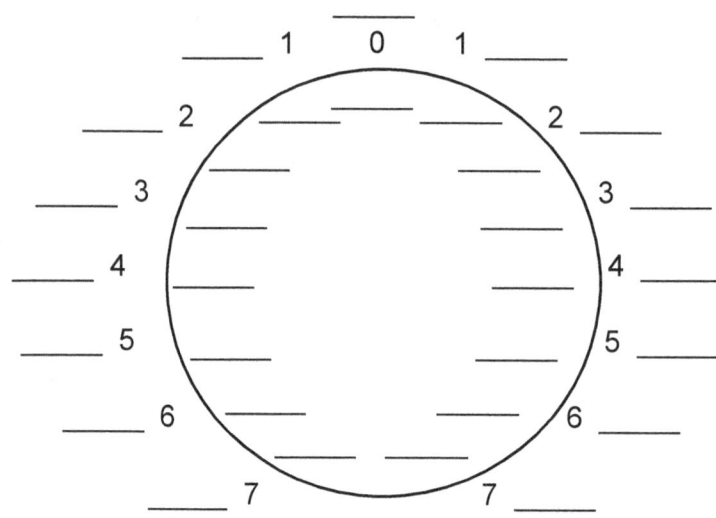

> ♪ **UMT Tip:** Begin by finding the Major or Perfect interval and then adjusting the lower (bottom) note to make the interval minor, diminished or Augmented.

1. a) Write the following harmonic intervals below each of the given notes. Use whole notes.

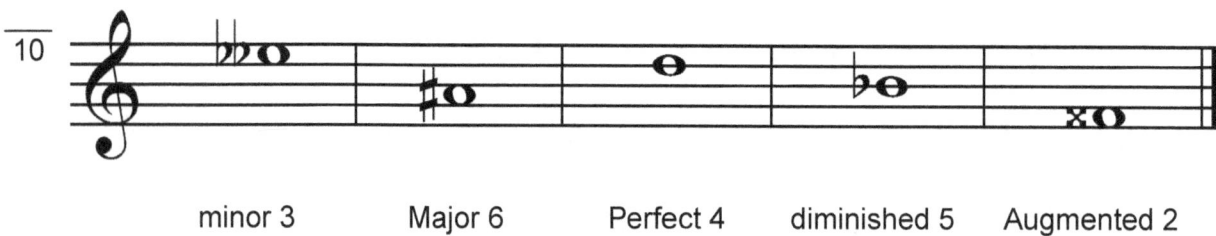

      minor 3   Major 6   Perfect 4   diminished 5   Augmented 2

b) Invert the above harmonic intervals in the given clef. Name the inversions.

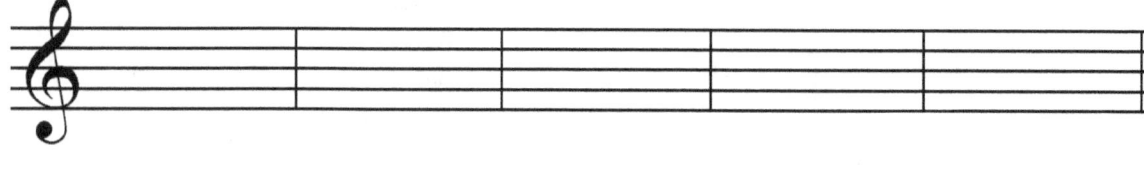

UltimateMusicTheory.com © Copyright 2013 Gloryland Publishing. All Rights Reserved.

ULTIMATE MUSIC THEORY
INTERMEDIATE EXAM SET #1 - EXAM #2

> ♪ **UMT Tip:** When writing a triad in first inversion or second inversion, first write it in root position in [square brackets] at the end of the measure. Then write the inversion at the beginning of the measure.

2. a) Write the following solid triads in close position in the Treble Clef. Use accidentals. Use whole notes.

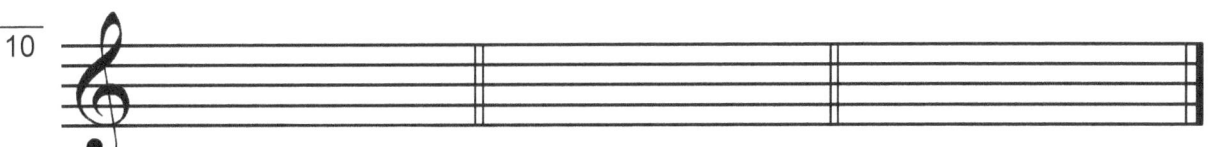

      Mediant triad of   Dominant triad of   Subdominant triad of
      B flat Major   D Major   g minor harmonic
      in second inversion   in root position   in first inversion

b) Write the following solid triads in close position in the Bass Clef. Use the correct Key Signature and any necessary accidentals. Use whole notes.

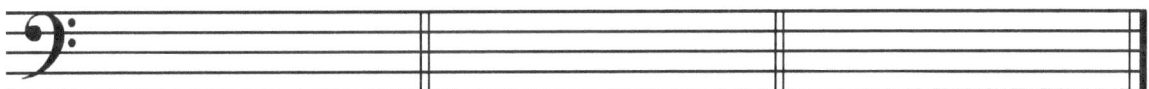

      Supertonic triad of   Submediant triad of   Subdominant triad of
      G flat Major   f sharp minor harmonic   A flat Major
      in first inversion   in second inversion   in root position

> ♪ **UMT Tip:** In open position, one note of the triad may be repeated. Rewrite the triad in root position in [square brackets] at the end of the measure. Use each note only once.

c) Identify the root note and the quality/type of each of the following open position triads.

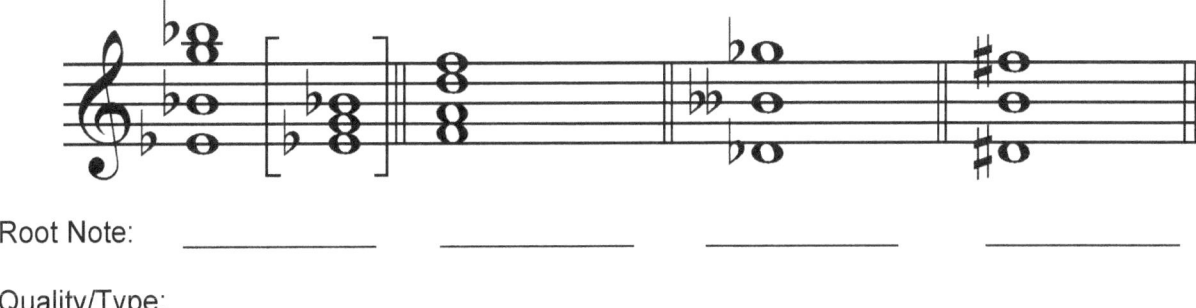

Root Note: _____ _____ _____ _____

Quality/Type: _____ _____ _____ _____

ULTIMATE MUSIC THEORY
INTERMEDIATE EXAM SET #1 - EXAM #2

> ♪ UMT Tip: When transposing a melody to a new key, a Major key will ALWAYS remain a Major key.

3. The following melody is in the key of E flat Major.
   a) Transpose the given melody UP an Augmented fourth. Use the correct Key Signature.
   b) Name the key of the new melody.

Key: E flat Major

Key: _____

> ♪ UMT Tip: Name the accidentals in order of the Key Signature. When accidentals are in the correct Key Signature order, the key is usually Major.

The following melody has been written using accidentals instead of a Key Signature.
c) Name the key of the given melody.
d) Rewrite the given melody using the correct Key Signature and any necessary accidentals.

Key: _____

UltimateMusicTheory.com © Copyright 2013 Gloryland Publishing. All Rights Reserved.

ULTIMATE MUSIC THEORY
INTERMEDIATE EXAM SET #1 - EXAM #2

> ♪ **UMT Tip:** Chromatic scale using any standard notation - starts and ends on the same Tonic note and does not use any letter name more than twice. Whole tone scale using any standard notation - starts and ends on the same Tonic note and uses the same notes and accidentals (all sharps or all flats) ascending and descending.

4. Write the following scales, ascending and descending, using accidentals. Use whole notes.

   10 a) Chromatic scale beginning on D in the Treble Clef. Use any standard notation.

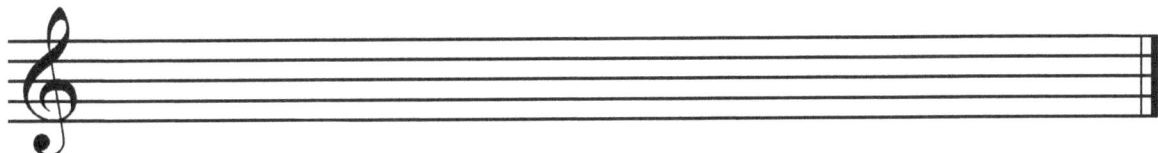

   b) Whole tone scale beginning on A flat in the Bass Clef. Use any standard notation.

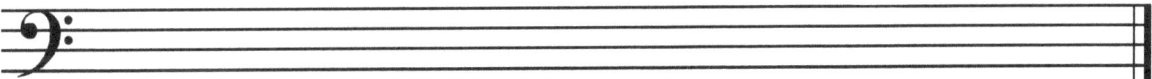

   c) Relative minor scale, harmonic form, of B Major in the Bass Clef.

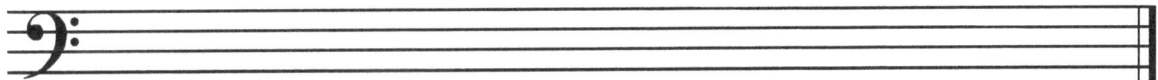

   d) Tonic minor scale, natural form, of F Major in the Treble Clef.

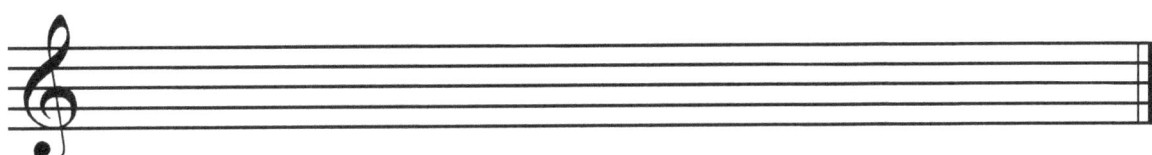

   e) Enharmonic Tonic Major scale of C sharp Major in the Bass Clef.

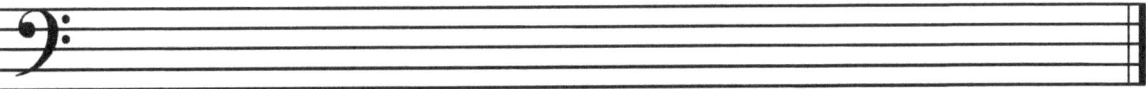

ULTIMATE MUSIC THEORY
INTERMEDIATE EXAM SET #1 - EXAM #2

> ♪ **UMT Tip:** Each Key Signature will have two options - the Major key and its relative minor key. Check to see if the final note is the Tonic or the Dominant note in the Major key or in the relative minor key.

5. For each of the following cadences, name:
   a) the key.
   b) the type of cadence (Perfect, Plagal or Imperfect).

Key: _____ _____ _____

Type: _____ _____ _____

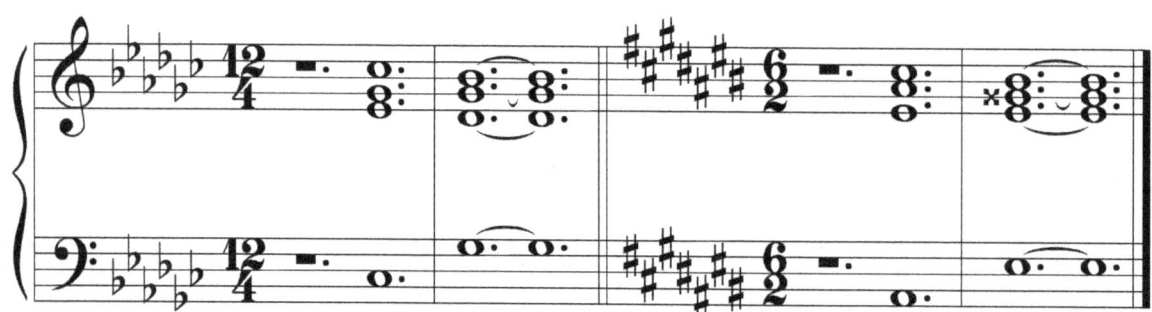

Key: _____ _____

Type: _____ _____

ULTIMATE MUSIC THEORY
INTERMEDIATE EXAM SET #1 - EXAM #2

> ♪ **UMT Tip:** Look for single notes or groups of 3 notes to determine whether the Time Signature is Simple Time or Compound Time.

6. For each of the following excerpts:
   a) Name the key.
   b) Add the correct Time Signature below the bracket.

Key: _____

Key: _____

Key: _____

Key: _____

Key: _____

ULTIMATE MUSIC THEORY
INTERMEDIATE EXAM SET #1 - EXAM #2

♪ **UMT Tip:** Write the Basic Beat and pulse below each measure. When indicating to JOIN pulses, use the "+" plus sign. When indicating to NOT join pulses use the "~" tilde sign.

7. Add rests below each bracket to complete each measure.

ULTIMATE MUSIC THEORY
INTERMEDIATE EXAM SET #1 - EXAM #2

♪ **UMT Tip:** Use the Circle of Fifths to identify the Key Signature.

8. a) Name the following notes.

   $\frac{}{10}$

   The Leading note of d minor harmonic is _____.

   The Mediant of G Major is _____.

   The Dominant of e minor melodic is _____.

   The Supertonic of C♯ Major is _____.

   The Submediant of b♭ minor melodic (ascending) is _____.

   b) For each of the following, name the minor key. Identify the technical degree name of the note.

minor key: _____ _____ _____

Technical
degree name: _____ _____ _____

minor key: _____ _____

Technical
degree name: _____ _____

UltimateMusicTheory.com © Copyright 2013 Gloryland Publishing. All Rights Reserved.

ULTIMATE MUSIC THEORY
INTERMEDIATE EXAM SET #1 - EXAM #2

> ♪ **UMT Tip:** Before looking at the possible definitions, look at the Term and identify the definition. Remember that not all definitions will be used.

9. Match each musical term with its English definition. (Not all definitions will be used.)

$\overline{10}$

Term		Definition
ma	_____	a) becoming quicker
con brio	_____	b) lightly
accelerando	_____	c) much, very
bene	_____	d) always, continuously
leggiero	_____	e) but
meno mosso	_____	f) well
molto	_____	g) expressive, with expression
più mosso	_____	h) without
sempre	_____	i) more movement, quicker
espressivo	_____	j) less movement, slower
		k) with vigor, spirit

UltimateMusicTheory.com © Copyright 2013 Gloryland Publishing. All Rights Reserved.

ULTIMATE MUSIC THEORY
INTERMEDIATE EXAM SET #1 - EXAM #2

> ♪ **UMT Tip:** The Time Signature is written in both the Treble Clef and the Bass Clef.

10. Analyze the following piece of music by answering the questions below.

Broken Cookies
S. McKibbon

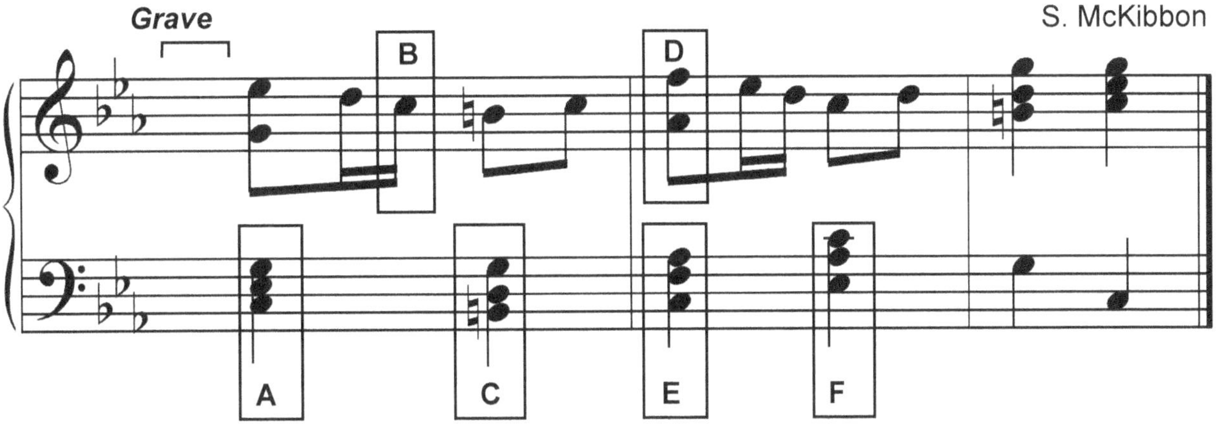

a) Name the key of this piece. _____

b) Explain the tempo of this piece. _____

c) Add the Time Signature directly on the music.

d) For the triad at **A**, name: Root: ____ Type/Quality: _____ Position: _____

e) Identify the technical degree of the note at the letter **B**. _____

f) For the triad at **C**, name: Root: ____ Type/Quality: _____ Position: _____

g) Name the interval at the letter **D**. _____

h) For the triad at **E**, name: Root: ____ Type/Quality: _____ Position: _____

i) For the triad at **F**, name: Root: ____ Type/Quality: _____ Position: _____

j) Identify the cadence in measure 3 as Perfect, Imperfect or Plagal. _____

UltimateMusicTheory.com © Copyright 2013 Gloryland Publishing. All Rights Reserved.

ULTIMATE MUSIC THEORY
INTERMEDIATE EXAM SET #1 - EXAM #3

Total Score: ____ / 100

1. a) Write the following harmonic intervals below each of the given notes. Use whole notes.

    diminished 3   Perfect 4   minor 6   Major 7   Augmented 5

b) Invert the above harmonic intervals in the same clef. Name the inversions. Use whole notes.

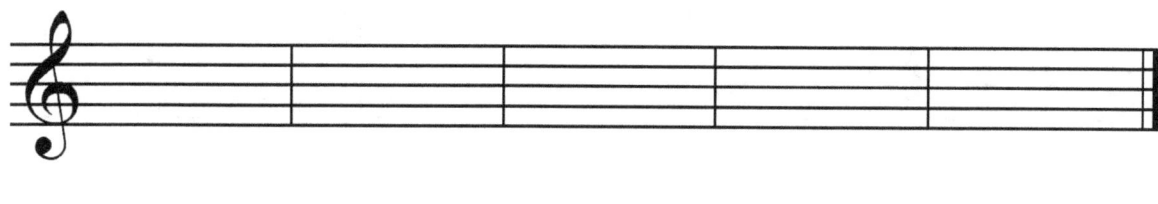

_____   _____   _____   _____   _____

c) Write the following melodic intervals above each of the given notes. Use whole notes.

    Augmented 2   diminished 5   Major 3   Perfect 8   Major 6

d) Invert the above melodic intervals in the same clef. Name the inversions. Use whole notes.

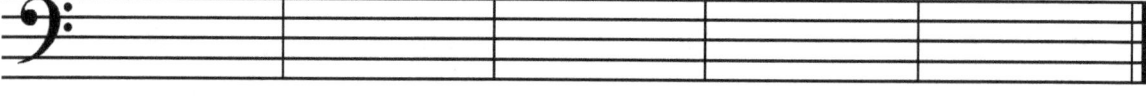

_____   _____   _____   _____   _____

UltimateMusicTheory.com © Copyright 2013 Gloryland Publishing. All Rights Reserved.

ULTIMATE MUSIC THEORY
INTERMEDIATE EXAM SET #1 - EXAM #3

2. Match each description in the left column with the correct solid triad, in close or in open position, in the right column.

10 Tonic triad of c minor
harmonic in first inversion   _____

Subdominant triad of f minor
harmonic in root position   _____

Mediant Triad of E Major
in second inversion   _____

Dominant triad of G Major
in second inversion   _____

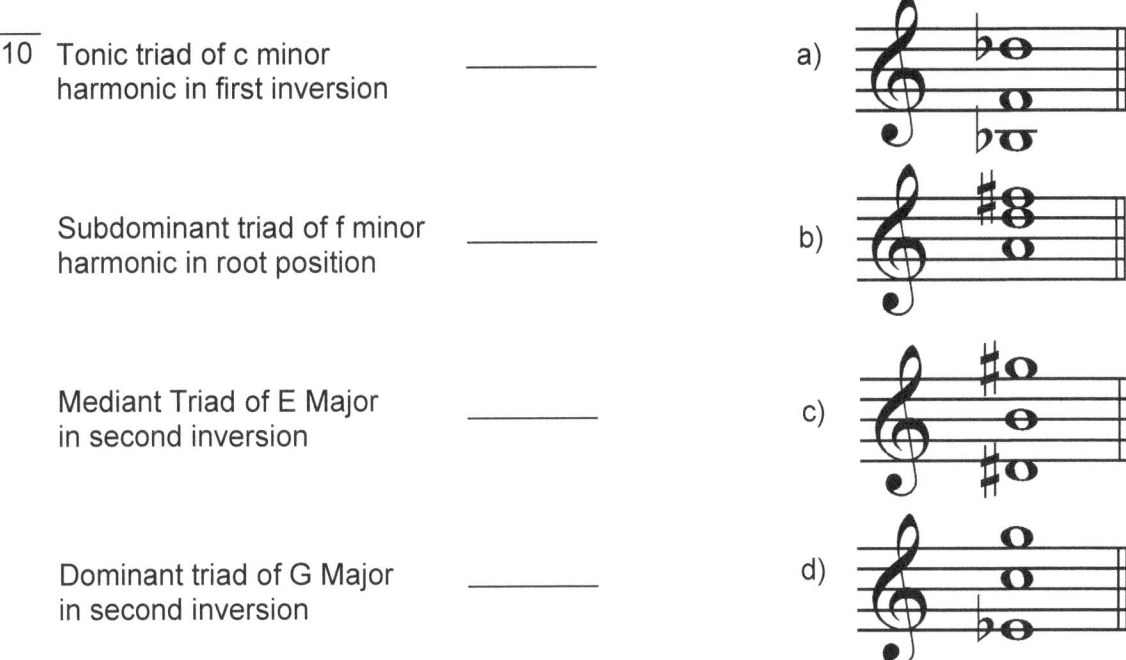

Write the following triads in close position and solid form. Use a Key Signature and any necessary accidentals. Use whole notes.

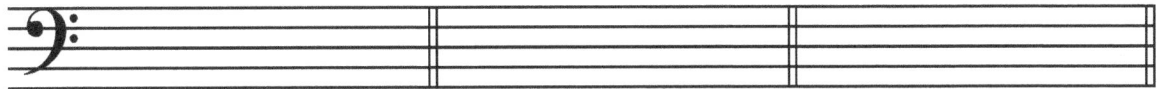

e) Supertonic triad of
D flat Major
in root position

f) Leading note triad of
c sharp minor harmonic
in first inversion

g) Submediant triad of
A Major
in second inversion

h) Tonic triad of
A flat Major
in root position

i) Mediant triad of
C sharp Major
in second inversion

j) Subdominant triad of
c minor harmonic
in first inversion

UltimateMusicTheory.com © Copyright 2012 Gloryland Publishing All Rights Reserved

ULTIMATE MUSIC THEORY
INTERMEDIATE EXAM SET #1 - EXAM #3

3. The following melody is in the key of A Major.
   a) Transpose the given melody UP a minor third. Use the correct Key Signature. Name the key of the new melody.
   b) Transpose the given melody UP a diminished fifth. Use the correct Key Signature. Name the key of the new melody.

Key: A Major

Key: _____

Key: _____

ULTIMATE MUSIC THEORY
INTERMEDIATE EXAM SET #1 - EXAM #3

4. Write the following scales, ascending and descending, in the given clefs. Use whole notes.

$\overline{10}$ a) The relative minor scale, melodic form, of C flat Major. Use accidentals.

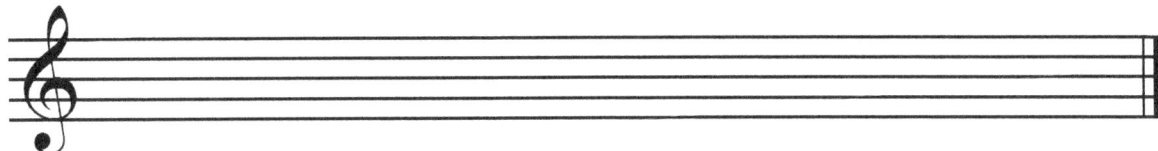

b) The Tonic minor scale, harmonic form, of B Major. Use a Key Signature.

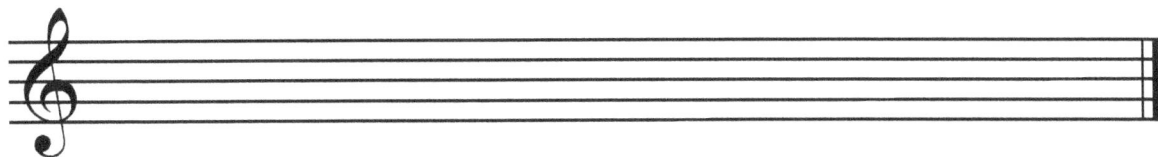

c) G flat Major scale. Use a Key Signature.

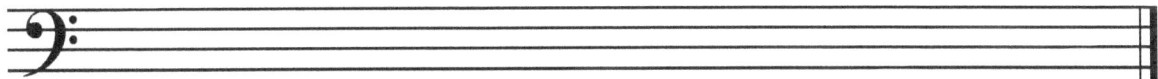

d) Whole Tone scale beginning on F. Use accidentals. Use any standard notation.

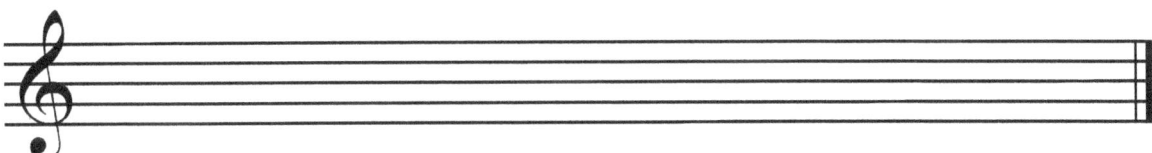

e) Chromatic scale beginning on G. Use accidentals. Use any standard notation.

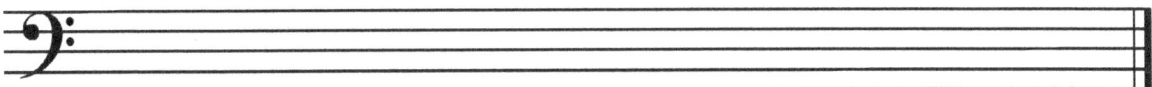

ULTIMATE MUSIC THEORY
INTERMEDIATE EXAM SET #1 - EXAM #3

5. For each of the following cadences, name:
   a) the key.
   b) the type of cadence (Perfect, Plagal or Imperfect).

<u>   </u>
10

Key: _____ _____ _____

Type: _____ _____ _____

Key: _____ _____

Type: _____ _____

UltimateMusicTheory.com © Copyright 2013 Gloryland Publishing. All Rights Reserved.

ULTIMATE MUSIC THEORY
INTERMEDIATE EXAM SET #1 - EXAM #3

6. For each of the following excerpts:
   a) Name the key.
   b) Add the correct Time Signature below the bracket.

10

Key: _____

Key: _____

Key: _____

Key: _____

Key: _____

UltimateMusicTheory.com © Copyright 2013 Gloryland Publishing. All Rights Reserved.

ULTIMATE MUSIC THEORY
INTERMEDIATE EXAM SET #1 - EXAM #3

7. Add rests below each bracket to complete each measure.

ULTIMATE MUSIC THEORY
INTERMEDIATE EXAM SET #1 - EXAM #3

8. For each of the following:
   a) Name the minor key.
   b) Identify the technical degree name for each note. (Do not use Roman Numerals or abbreviations.)

___
10

a) _____   _____   _____

b) _____   _____   _____

a) _____   _____   _____

b) _____   _____   _____

b) Name the following scales as blues, chromatic, Major pentatonic, minor pentatonic, octatonic or whole tone.

ULTIMATE MUSIC THEORY
INTERMEDIATE EXAM SET #1 - EXAM #3

9. For each of the following Italian Terms, circle whether the definition is True or False.

$\frac{}{10}$

Term	Definition	True or False
troppo	too much	**(True)** or False
senza	with	True or False
sempre	much, very much	True or False
molto	without	True or False
non	not	True or False
meno	less	True or False
ma	but	True or False
alla	in the manner of	True or False
ed	and	True or False
ben	well	True or False
colle	little	True or False

UltimateMusicTheory.com © Copyright 2013 Gloryland Publishing. All Rights Reserved.

ULTIMATE MUSIC THEORY
INTERMEDIATE EXAM SET #1 - EXAM #3

10. Analyze the following piece of music by answering the questions below.

Layla's Waltz

S. McKibbon

Allegretto

a) Name the key of this piece. _____

b) Explain the tempo of this piece. _____

c) Add the Time Signature directly on the music.

d) Explain the number at the letter **A**. _____

e) Identify the cadence in measure 2 as Perfect, Plagal or Imperfect. _____

f) Name the intervals at the following letters: **B** _____ **C** _____

g) Identify the cadence in measure 4 as Perfect, Plagal or Imperfect. _____

h) Circle a diatonic semitone in this piece. Label it as d.s.

i) How many measures are in this piece? _____

j) Explain the sign at the letter **D**. _____

ULTIMATE MUSIC THEORY
INTERMEDIATE EXAM SET #1 - EXAM #4

Total Score: ___
100

1. a) Name the following harmonic intervals.

___ ___ ___ ___ ___

b) Invert the above harmonic intervals in the same clef. Name the inversions.

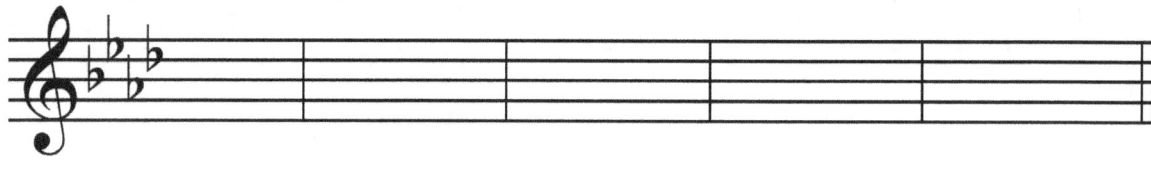

___ ___ ___ ___ ___

c) Name the following melodic intervals.

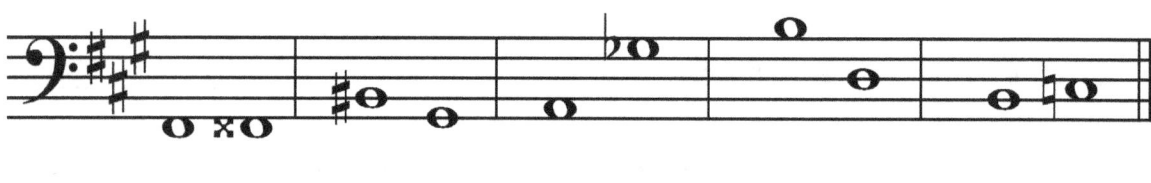

___ ___ ___ ___ ___

d) Invert the above melodic intervals in the same clef. Name the inversions.

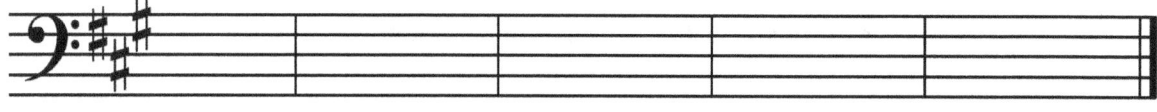

___ ___ ___ ___ ___

ULTIMATE MUSIC THEORY
INTERMEDIATE EXAM SET #1 - EXAM #4

2. Match each description in the left column with the correct solid triad, in close or in open position, in the right column.

Subdominant triad of e minor harmonic in first inversion	c	a)
Tonic triad of E flat Major in second inversion	_____	b)
Submediant triad of a sharp minor harmonic in root position	_____	c)
Mediant triad of D Major in second inversion	_____	d)
Dominant triad of a minor harmonic in first inversion	_____	e)
Tonic triad of f minor harmonic in root position	_____	f)
Subdominant triad of E Major in second inversion	_____	g)
Supertonic triad of C Major in root position	_____	h)
Tonic triad of a flat minor harmonic in first inversion	_____	i)
Dominant triad of d sharp minor harmonic in root position	_____	j)
Submediant triad of F sharp Major in second inversion	_____	k)

(10)

UltimateMusicTheory.com © Copyright 2013 Gloryland Publishing. All Rights Reserved.

ULTIMATE MUSIC THEORY
INTERMEDIATE EXAM SET #1 - EXAM #4

3. The following melody is in the key of A flat Major.
   a) Transpose the given melody UP a Major second. Use the correct Key Signature. Name the key of the new melody.
   b) Transpose the given melody UP an Augmented fifth. Use the correct Key Signature. Name the key of the new melody.

Key: A flat Major

Key: _____

Key: _____

ULTIMATE MUSIC THEORY
INTERMEDIATE EXAM SET #1 - EXAM #4

4. Write the following scales, ascending and descending, in the given clefs. Use whole notes.

a) The enharmonic relative minor scale, harmonic form, of F sharp Major. Use accidentals.

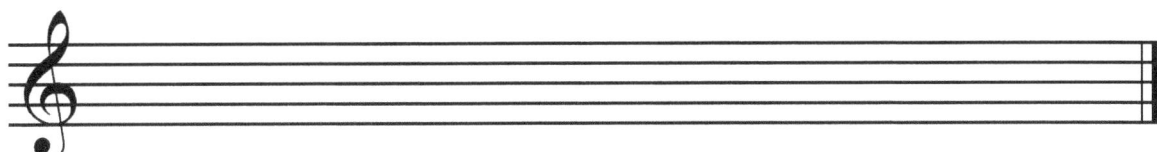

b) The Tonic minor scale, melodic form, of E Major. Use a Key Signature.

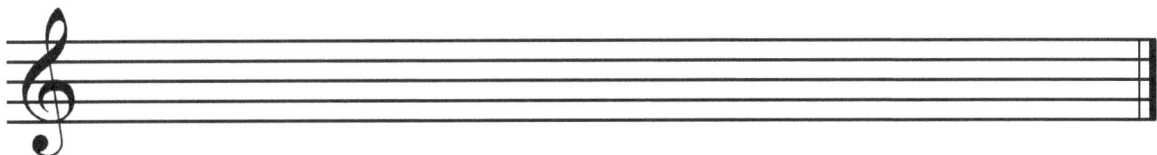

c) A flat Major scale. Use a Key Signature.

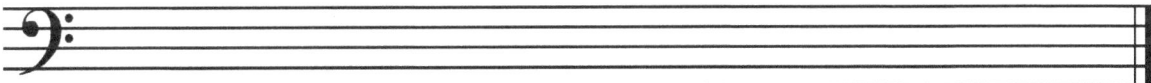

d) Whole Tone scale beginning on B flat. Use accidentals. Use any standard notation.

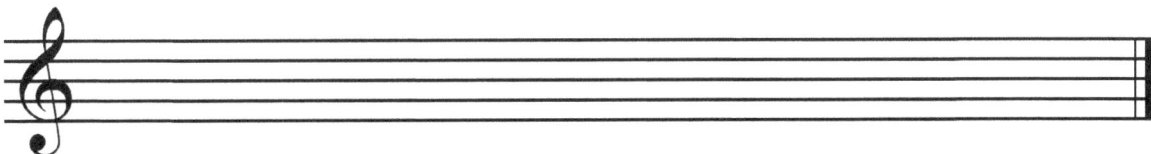

e) Chromatic scale beginning on B. Use accidentals. Use any standard notation.

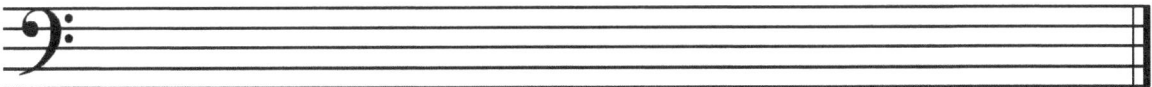

ULTIMATE MUSIC THEORY
INTERMEDIATE EXAM SET #1 - EXAM #4

5. For each of the following cadences, name:
   a) the key.
   b) the type of cadence (Perfect, Plagal or Imperfect).

Key: _____ _____ _____

Type: _____ _____ _____

Key: _____ _____

Type: _____ _____

ULTIMATE MUSIC THEORY
INTERMEDIATE EXAM SET #1 - EXAM #4

6. For each of the following excerpts:
   a) Name the key.
   b) Add the correct Time Signature below the bracket.

10

Key: _____

Key: _____

Key: _____

Key: _____

Key: _____

ULTIMATE MUSIC THEORY
INTERMEDIATE EXAM SET #1 - EXAM #4

7. Add rests below each bracket to complete each measure.

ULTIMATE MUSIC THEORY
INTERMEDIATE EXAM SET #1 - EXAM #4

8. For each of the following:
   a) Name the minor key.
   b) Identify the technical degree name for each note. (Do not use Roman Numerals or abbreviations.)

___
10

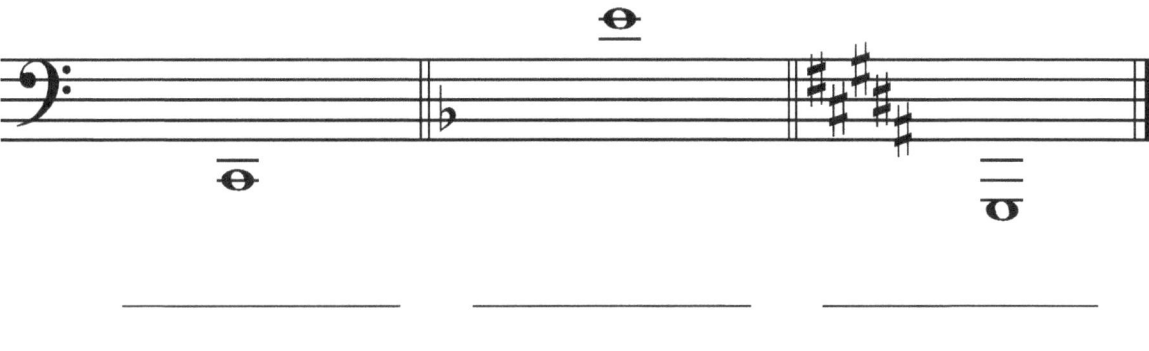

a) _____   _____   _____

b) _____   _____   _____

a) _____   _____

b) _____   _____

c) Name the following notes.

   The Submediant of F Major is _____.

   The Tonic of A flat Major is _____.

   The Subdominant of C sharp Major is _____.

   The Leading note of G flat Major is _____.

   The Supertonic of B flat Major is _____.

ULTIMATE MUSIC THEORY
INTERMEDIATE EXAM SET #1 - EXAM #4

9. For each of the following Italian Terms, circle whether the definition is True or False.

___/10

Term	Definition	True or False
non troppo	not too much	**True** or False
con espressione	with vigor, spirit	True or False
assai	much, very much	True or False
col	with	True or False
animato	quiet, tranquil	True or False
poco	little	True or False
tre corde	three strings; release the left (piano) pedal	True or False
una corda	one string; depress the left (piano) pedal	True or False
grave	graceful	True or False
senza	without	True or False
leggiero	softly	True or False

ULTIMATE MUSIC THEORY
INTERMEDIATE EXAM SET #1 - EXAM #4

10. Analyze the following excerpt by answering the questions below.

Ecossaise

Ludwig van Beethoven

a) Name the key of this piece. _____

b) Explain the tempo of this piece. _____

c) Add the Time Signature directly on the music.

d) Explain the term at the letter **A**. _____

e) Add the correct rest at the letter **B**.

f) For the triad at **C**, name: Root: _____ Type/Quality: _____ Position: _____

g) Explain the sign at the letter **D**. _____

h) Name the intervals at the following letters: E _____ F _____

i) Circle a chromatic semitone in this piece. Label it as c.s.

j) How many measures are in this excerpt? _____

Workbooks, Exams, Answers, Online Courses, App & More!

A Proven Step-by-Step System to Learn Theory Faster - from Beginner to Advanced.

Innovative techniques designed to develop a complete understanding of music theory, to enhance sight reading, ear training, creativity, composition and musical expression.

All UMT Series have matching Answer Books!

The UMT Rudiments Series - Beginner A, Beginner B, Beginner C, Prep 1, Prep 2, Basic, Intermediate, Advanced & Complete (All-In-One)

- ♪ 12 Lessons, Review Tests, and a Final Exam to develop confidence
- ♪ Music Theory Guide & Chart for fast and easy reference of theory concepts
- ♪ 80 Flashcards for fun drills to dramatically increase retention & comprehension

Rudiments Exam Series - Preparatory, Basic, Intermediate & Advanced

- ♪ 8 Exams plus UMT Tips on How to Score 100% on Theory Exams

Each Rudiments Workbook correlates to a Supplemental Workbook.

The UMT Supplemental Series - Prep Level, Level 1, Level 2, Level 3, Level 4, Level 5, Level 6, Level 7, Level 8 & Complete (All-In-One) Level

- ♪ Form & Analysis and Music History - Composers, Eras & Musical Styles
- ♪ Melody Writing using ICE - Imagine, Compose & Explore
- ♪ 12 Lessons, Review Tests, Final Exam and 80 Flashcards for quick study

Supplemental Exam Series - Level 5, Level 6, Level 7 & Level 8

- ♪ 8 Exams to successfully prepare for nationally recognized Theory Exams

UMT Online Courses, Music Theory App & More

- ♪ UMT Certification Course, Teachers Membership & Elite Educator Program
- ♪ Ultimate Music Theory App correlates to the Rudiments Workbooks
- ♪ Free Resources - Teachers Guide, Music Theory Blogs, videos & downloads

Go To: **UltimateMusicTheory.com**

www.ingramcontent.com/pod-product-compliance
Lightning Source LLC
Chambersburg PA
CBHW081735100526
44591CB00016B/2626